T0272731

Mark Wheeller

Chequered Flags to Chequered Futures

A Verbatim Play

Revised and Updated (2020)

Commissioned by the Victoria Shanghai Academy Hong Kong.

Salamander Street

PLAYS

Chequered Flags to Chequered Futures published by Zinc Communicate in 2014
ISBN 9781902843339

This edition first published in 2020 by Salamander Street Ltd.,
272 Bath Street, Glasgow, G2 4JR (info@salamanderstreet.com)

PB ISBN: 9781913630355
E ISBN: 9781913630348

Cover and text design by Konstantinos Vasdekis

10 9 8 7 6 5 4 3 2 1

Further copies of this publication can be purchased from
www.salamanderstreet.com

CONTENTS

Acknowledgements

Chris, Lucy, Bryoni, Ann & Roy Gilfoy. Jane and Shelley Halsey. Graham Ings for their words and permission to use this emotive story.

Rachael, Ollie and Daisy, my family, who have to put up with my commitment to writing and then developing these plays.

Joanna Crimmins, Jeremy Otto, Richard Parker from Victoria Shanghai Academy who gave me the opportunity to "get on with it".

ISTA (International Schools' Theatre Association) for basing a whole conference around the premiere of this play.

Thanks to Ten Alps Communicate (later known as Zinc Publishing) who originally made this play available to schools when others would not have done so.

Thanks to George Spender and those in the Salamander Street team for their efforts to extend the reach of my plays.

Sophie Gorell Barnes and all at MBA for their continued support and belief.

Introduction

I was certain *Driven to Distraction* (2009), my would also be my final one road safety play. Arguably it was, as this is no message laden "road safety" play at all. It uses an avoidable Road Traffic Accident (RTA) as the tragic centrepiece to true story of three young lives suddenly torpedoed into a different trajectory.

The huge impact *Too Much Punch For Judy* had, led to my being commissioned to write all of the others. *Driven to Distraction* was no exception but was commissioned for a professional cast, unlike the others which were, initially, written for school age students.

I wanted to write a more naturalistic play and came up with an interesting structure counterpointing two time frames and two accounts of different parts of one story. Both parts collide at the end in the accident scene. The structure of *Driven to Distraction* inspired the one I use in *Chequered Flags* a few years on, where Chris's back story is longer and therefore faster but, once in hospital they catch up with each other.

I remember thinking...

   "I will never write another play with a road accident in it!"

(Just for the record... there was another one after this, as one of the characters referred to a horrific accident in my David Bowie tribute play *Can You Hear Me Major Tom?*)

A few years after I made that private pledge, I heard that an ex student/OYT member Chris Gilfoy (with whom I'd remained vaguely in touch), had been seriously injured in a tragic, real life car accident. Chris returned to OYT as part of his recovery. We came to know one another again and more than once, the idea of using his story as the basis for a play crossed my mind. I dismissed it and certainly didn't tell Chris my private thoughts (he will only discover them as he reads this!). I was concerned it might appear like I had some sort of weird obsession!

One day, I heard some students raving about a powerful talk they'd heard in a PSHE lesson from… yes you've guessed… Chris Gilfoy. They were saying what a powerful impact his story had made on them and, at that point, the weird obsession (I do clearly have) surfaced and I approached Chris. He told me the full story. It had inherent drama and was very different from all the other RTA "message" plays I'd written before.

I had begun to question the validity of propaganda plays since "Judy", the subject of *Too Much Punch for Judy*, had gone on to drink/drive (and kill another driver as a result) again. This situation raised the question:

If the person who perpetrated the offence doesn't learn from it how can I expect an audience watching the play do so?

I would write Chris's story without any pressure to adhere to pre-defined road safety messages. I would write it as the human tragedy it had been for all of those involved.

Chris had been involved as a twelve-year-old in developing *Chicken!* (giving his name to the lead character and his mum's (Ann) to his character's mum), so he was well aware of my back catalogue but was still surprised when I approached him:

> *When Mark first approached me about the possibility of our story being written as a play I was shocked. I didn't think it would be of interest to anyone else, but I knew that if it was going to happen then Mark would do a good job of it!*

After securing Chris's consent I made contact with Shelley, the driver and Jane, Shelley's mum, and was relieved to learn they were also willing for me to develop a verbatim play.

I conducted interviews with Jane and Shelley, Chris, his wife Lucy, his mum (Ann) and Dad (Roy). Then the problems began. I found it so hard to make time to transcribe the interviews. I had hours of tapes but the prospect seemed like a never-ending job. I delayed. More than a year passed and I had made no real progress. There was always another project for me to complete.

Then something utterly incredible happened. A fairy godmother landed. A fairy godmother from the other side of the world!

I went to Hong Kong to conduct a series of workshops in a school where my plays are studied. (Unbeknown to me, it seems my plays are used a lot in International School Drama Departments.) During the visit I was invited to a meal with two drama teachers from the Victoria Shanghai Academy. By the end of the meal they had invited their Principal, Richard Parker, to the meal and he asked me to think of a play I had always wanted to write... adding that their Academy would commission me to write it! I suggested Chris's story and said what an impact premiering this story would have on everyone... especially if Chris was able to attend the premiere!

From that point on everything moved unbelievably fast. I remember arriving home and transcribing the tapes well before any agreements had been finalised. Arrangements were made for the visit with four members of my Oasis Youth Theatre (performing a hastily rehearsed *Chicken!* as a partner play) securing an invitation too! What an opportunity! When I first told the Principal (at Oasis) and the young people in the cast, I don't think any of them believed it would happen. Their parents didn't either!

I completed an interview with Graham (the other passenger in the car) who I had made no effort to contact up until this point. I also interviewed Bryoni (who was in my Year 10 Drama Class), Chris and Lucy's daughter.

Around this time, verbatim theatre was gaining a credibility I never felt it had previously. I felt (perhaps wrongly) that it was regarded as second class. This genre wasn't viewed as "proper theatre" and so, I couldn't be considered a "proper writer" until I had created a successful naturalistic play... hence my determination to write one. Suddenly, I was being regarded as one of the elder statesmen of this "newly accepted' form. This was all magnificent for my confidence in writing this play, which uses the original words and virtually nothing "invented".

A few months later, I sent the first draft to VSA. They didn't ask for any changes. Everyone was delighted with the result. The title was developed through a Facebook thread in which all sorts of titles were suggested and discussed.

Chequered Flags to Chequered Futures was born.

The premiere was planned for October 2014. I was not involved in the development of the VSA performance, but had a strong impression that I had handed my play to a very confident drama department and put my trust in their professionalism. When we arrived in Hong Kong they were at dress rehearsal stage. Chris (who, with his family, was invited too) recalls watching that rehearsal:

When the time came to finally watch it being rehearsed and then performed in Hong Kong I was very nervous, and in fact when I saw it I was an emotional wreck!

I was sat next to Chris who was sobbing towards the end… and this was only the dress rehearsal! I remember putting my arm around him and he said:

It's all good. If I'm crying… it means it's good!

His presence lifted the performance of the cast beyond anything their teachers had expected.

The performances were incredibly powerful. A cast, all of whom had English as a second or third language, were speaking these colloquial words with obvious understanding and moving the audience to tears. It will live in my memory forever. Chris and his family participated in a Q&A, all of which is captured on film and that added such an invaluable dimension to this unique production.

Watching the play, there were only two minor amendments I chose to make. On occasions, I have to do so much re-writing but this seemed to have been "right" from the outset.

Although a commission, it was still a labour of love. It is one of only two plays where I knew the subject before I started the research, the other being *Sweet FA/No Place for a Girl*.

It also benefitted substantially from my developed understanding of structure which arrived in my head care of a John Burgess playwrighting course at the Nuffield Theatre in Southampton. He also delivered some classes on verbatim, which was the beginning of my accepting it as "officially sanctioned"!

The newfound confidence I have in the verbatim form shines through in this play. I had the confidence to use Jane's powerful monologues, as in her original interviews with me, without trying to break the speeches down into shorter lines spoken by different characters, which I may well have done previously to make it more like a play.

In the Hong Kong performance, we (in the audience) were able to prepare ourselves mentally, as Jane approached centre stage, for what we, (the audience) knew would be another harrowing account. It offered an effective change of pace to the lively ensemble approach that typified the way I dramatised Chris's story. (In the VSA production the ensemble were also used behind Jane to offer visual images to great effect.)

Now the play is published and will, we hope, develop a life of its own. I can't wait to see how it is used and whether, as I predict, it will eventually replace *Too Much Punch for Judy* as the favoured Mark Wheeller Road play featuring an avoidable RTA. I hope it will.

The thought of other schools performing our story is a bit surreal but I hope that a lesson can be learnt from the whole experience.

Mark Wheeller (with Chris Gilfoy)

Afterword 2020

I have been fortunate enough to witness two productions of *CFTCF* since its publication. Both were stunning.

The first was presented by professional director, Tim Ford, with a group from his Youth Theatre at the Hexagon Theatre in Reading. Tim had presented a number of my plays and so was a bit of an expert.

He brought a big difference to the production as he had a much more detailed setting rather than the black box space used at VSA. I remember walking into the studio theatre and being greeted by a cast dressed predominantly in overalls as would be seen on a race track or mechanics. If that wasn't enough to throw us into the theme of the play he had a variety of car parts hanging from the rig and discarded tyres adorning the stage area. The performance, which was seen by Shelley and Jane (for the first time) was as stunning as I remember it in Hong Kong. Sadly it received no coverage, so it remains in my memory and those few others who saw it…

The second production was by The Samuel Ward School (now Academy) in Haverhill. It was outstanding. Like Tim, Matt Russell is an expert on directing my plays as he does one of mine every a year! I filmed some moments of their dress rehearsal and often feature them on my Wheellerplays Facebook and Twitter pages. The opening to their production was one of the most dynamic openings I've seen for any play… and I'm embarrassed to say that they ignored the opening I had in the original Zinc text, and developed one they thought should be there in a proper Wheellerplay about a successful banger racer. You can now see my version of theirs, adapted in this version of the script. Thanks, Matt for the idea! I am also delighted that Matt has agreed to write about his approach to this play as a director. (See the next page.)

Of all the plays I have written this one has most frustrated me. It has become a perpetual and needlessly well kept secret. I hope the opportunity arising from Salamander Street publishing it, along with my better known scripts, will bring it into a focus that will encourage people to explore it more fully.

Mark Wheeller

From Page to Stage with Matt Russell

I first met Mark back in 2014 for our production of *Too Much Punch for Judy*. We have been lucky enough to produce a Mark Wheeller play every year since and continue to do so without fail. His texts are a perfect guide to developing the skills of drama teachers all over the country, who are at different stages in their career and are passionate about developing their creative skills as directors. Mark's texts are predominantly written in a verbatim style which gives the cast and the director a point of focus. The themes that surround these true stories are the nucleus, however the way in which drama 'teacher/directors' can stage them is down to interpretation and is an outstanding way to push creative decisions to new and exciting ends.

CFTCF is a perfect example. This production is heavily reliant on some lengthy and beautiful monologues. Although this could potentially make rehearsals tougher for a larger cast, you will soon realise that the chorus can offer vital stage presence in regards to tableaux, symbolic movement and choral speaking. Personally, I found rehearsals, at times, very intense. The actors, even though they were thoroughly enjoying the process, appeared deeply moved by the story and were inspired by the creative opportunities each scene offered. However, this directly leads onto a hugely relevant point, which are the sorts of things a young cast could be thinking about when exploring such a text. You can always step back as a young actor and look at large professional sets, lighting rigs, sound design etc, marvel at the complexity of them all and think 'big' in order to capture the vastness of it all. Alternatively, you can think on a smaller, much more personal level that encourages our young performers to look into elements of symbolism that could somehow make intelligent and relevant connections to the characters' story or 'place' within the text.

We decided to take this approach during the table read and early pre-production meetings. I remember sitting with the cast, showing them rough sketches I had drawn, set pieces and playing them pieces of music to see what they thought. The atmosphere was positively electric and the general consensus was to keep things simple, symbolic and impactful. We didn't want to make any changes to the text, the thought never crossed my mind. However, I did look at the opening from a different perspective. In the original script for *CFTCF* we see a flashback of Chris Gilfroy in one of his drama classes, being the centre of attention and generally enjoying some activities and improvisations, something he was clearly very talented in. Mark's stage directions call for the action to be fast-paced and gripping with a clear undertone of humour which gives the audience a calming perspective into the nature of Chris's humane persona. I loved reading this scene but secretly felt as if it needed something different, something that resonated with the tone and atmosphere we were trying to create.

I remember researching Chris's story and thinking that it was his goal to achieve big in his ambition as a professional driver. Having been the world's number one champion banger racer in 2000, surely more was on the cards. Clearly the accident in 2006 cut it short, so that's where the 're-imagining' of our interpretation started.

The cast and I constructed 20 1ft x 1ft wooden squares and painted them black and white to resemble a large chequered flag. This represented the end goal, or pinnacle, of Chris's career. It was clear that, had this accident not happened, Chris's life as a professional driver could have taken off in a very different direction. We wanted the flag to be easily dismantled to help represent this.

Our re-imagined opening shows an empty stage, littered with these wooden segments, the cast enter and with a physicalised movement, pick them up and slowly form the flag. As the music enters a crescendo, two cast members hit the centre of the flag disintegrating it. This cue also triggered a small blast from the smoke machine and some strong back lighting which, whilst the segments of flag were lowed to the floor, reveal a penitent looking Shelly, played by Grace Clancy. The opening continues with the cast placing the wooden squares along the front of the stage in a straight line which we had decided would represent the timeline of the play, leading up to the devastating decisions made by Chris and his two friends. The opening closes with the chorus recreating the crash in slow-motion whilst using Greek unison to heighten the impact.

In November of 2017, we invited Mark and Chris to come and see our production of *CFTCF*. Our guests were kind enough to stay for the day and work with the cast and take part in a Q&A session with the audience at the end of the final night. Chris really opened up during the session and was able to share the most difficult parts of his experience of the crash whilst maintaining a calm and admirable composure. This clearly resonated with the audience. What was even more inspiring was the close bond that Chris formed with our lead actor Wez Ruthven who played Chris in our production. They stayed in touch regularly for the months that followed with Wez constantly taking advice from Chris in order to develop his performance even more in preparation for our admission into the Cambridge Drama Festival in May 2018.

This experience really brought out the commitment of our young cast and Mark Wheeller's wonderful story has brought out the best in all of them. Working on this production was a pleasure and I hope anyone that attempts to recreate it will treasure a similar experience.

Chequered Flags to Chequered Futures was commissioned by the Victoria Shanghai Academy and was first performed there in October 2014 with the following cast:

Ryan Tang, Lorianne Ho, Stephanie Wong, Megumi Pang, Hok Hin Ng, Brian Hung, Rex Yiu, Britney To, Anson Ng, Megan Ng, Kimberly Chow, Donna Wong, Katherine Wong, Harry Mou, Ashley Ho, Tiffany Lau, Sabrina Yu.

It was directed by Joanna Crimmins and assisted by Ellie Mockler and Jeremy Sampson.

Characters

CHRIS

LUCY
Chris's wife

ANN
Chris's mum

ROY
Chris's dad

BRYONI
Chris's daughter

JANE

SHELLEY
Jane's daughter and Chris's friend

GRAHAM
Friend of both Chris and Shelley

ACTOR

WITNESS

DRIVER OF THE RENAULT

POLICE OFFICER

There is the opportunity within the play for a Chorus to be present representing people, feelings, events and objects. I hope that by using a Chorus the performance will become more imaginative and innovative.

CHRIS'S STORY 1

Music plays as lights gradually fade up on a stage which is littered with 20 1ft x 1ft wooden squares painted black (10) and white (10). The cast enter and with a stylised movement to represent ambition and determination, they each pick a square up and move to the front of the stage to form a vertical chequered flag.

The underscored music crescendos as two cast members hit the centre of the flag (in slow motion) forming it to disintegrate, again in slow motion. This cue also triggered a small blast from the smoke machine and some strong back lighting which, whilst the segments of flag are lowered to the floor, reveal a penitent-looking **SHELLEY**. *The cast place the wooden squares along the front of the stage in a straight line which represent not only the chequered start line of a race track but the timeline of the play, leading up to the devastating decisions made by* **CHRIS**, **GRAHAM** *and* **SHELLEY**. *The opening closes with the chorus recreating the crash in slow-motion with* **ANN** *and* **ROY** *looking on and reacting with horror, to heighten the impact with the three central characters in their respective places in the car. As they complete this* **BRYONI** *emerges from the scene showing she has been one of the central performers in the scene. She speaks, indicating* **CHRIS**, *as the rest of the cast continue in a tableau or slow motion supportive action.* **CHRIS**, **ANN**, **ROY** *&* **ACTOR** *all leave the scene as it becomes their turn to speak[1].*

BRYONI: When I started doing drama at secondary school my dad always told me the history of when he was there. "I done this, I done that," and it's like "Oh God!" Oh, and "I got an A*". *(Laughs)*

CHRIS: At secondary school I loved drama... liked to make people laugh.

ANN: He could just pick up something and make it funny.

CHRIS: I'd walk through them theatre doors and it was like we was somewhere else.

It started through Mum *(Indicates* **ANN**.*),* who worked there. I used to go from junior school to get a lift home and sat in the little spinney chairs in her office, spinning myself around for hours.

ANN: *(Laughing)* If he was looking at a poster, say about badminton, he'd be there trying to do the actions of a badminton player.

CHRIS: One day I saw a poster for OYT auditions. I thought, "I'll have a go at that," I never realised I'd get into it as heavily as I did.

---

1   Credit to Matthew Russell and his production at The Samuel Ward School (now Academy) who provided Mark with the inspiration to use his introduction to the play rather than what appeared in the original publication.

ANN: We had an idea he'd be good because he was very… erm I don't know quite what the word would be but…

ROY: He was comical.

ANN: Yes.

ROY: … and he's still like it.

CHRIS: I made so many friends.

ANN: I remember him coming home one day and saying, I'm going to help Mark, his drama teacher, to write a play. I said, "Oh what's that?" And he said:

CHRIS: It's going to be called "Why Did the Chicken Cross the Road?"

ANN: *(Laughing)* And I went "What?"

BRYONI: Yeh, he's always saying: "I wrote a play with Mark Wheeller!"

CHRIS: It was a road safety play… went on to tour all over the UK.

ROY: It was comical wasn't it?

ANN: It was sad, Roy.

ROY: Some of it was funny.

ANN: It was down to earth.

ROY: Yeh.

CHRIS: I went to see the professional group do it after we did it and when the rhyming speech at the end came I was mouthing all the words.

ACTOR: People'd say I'd encouraged her with a dare. They'd make judgements and suspect I didn't care
They'd say I should have known better… should have been more mature.
But everyone knows… for a moment's stupidity there is no known cure.

CHRIS: After all those years I remembered it word for word! It's ironic how I was part of this road safety play and… well… what's happened to me now.

ANN: It's very similar isn't it? Taking risks.

CHRIS: As much as drama was a passion, motor racing was something I'd always done and when the opportunities came of going abroad with it I thought, this is serious. There never was a moment where I decided not to do drama, just where I couldn't do it.

JANE: Right… going back to May 2007… it was the FA Cup Final, Chelsea v Man U. John and I went out for lunch with some friends and got back early afternoon to watch the match. Shelley was at home in the morning with me. She was meeting up with some old friends so, when she left, I said:

See you later,

…and that was it.

She was watching the match in the pub and she phoned her dad to sort of say… they were having a bit of banter. I just remember her dad laughing and saying… "Well we're off now, Shell…" 'cos we were going out with friends… we were off to speedway 'cos my son, Danny, is a speedway rider.

John, Danny and Stewart stayed in the pits, you know, to get the bike organised and everything.

My friend and I went up to the bar at the speedway track. We were stood there having a drink and I saw Danny and Kayleigh, his girlfriend… I could just tell by the way they were walking that something had gone down… something had happened. Danny said:

"There's been a bad accident in Wing and *(Voice breaks.)* I think Shelley was driving."

CHRIS'S STORY 2

CHRIS: Motorsport was my life if you know what I mean? I've always been involved, since I was a baby... literally when I was born, my dad raced grass track motorcycles and we'd go literally every weekend from March 'til November... every weekend in a different part of the country, racing bikes.

ANN: When I met Roy, in 1979, one of the things he made clear to me was that his first love was motor racing.

ROY: All of a sudden, erm, I was asked to have my kids from my first marriage, and Ann said:

ANN: That's all right. Go and get them. I'll have them.

ROY: Ann, I need you to know. My first love is racing. I go racing a lot. I just...

ANN: Don't worry, Roy. Just go and get them.

ROY: We went over and got them, didn't we? It was a Thursday night. I'll never forget it. Ann took them on. We ended up a big family overnight, which was good wasn't it?

ANN: We do prattle on a bit and get off the subject don't we?

CHRIS: Dad had a bad accident and had to retire, but we kept going 'cos he became Ken Layne's mechanic. Ken's one of the most successful ever grass track 1000 cc. motor-bike and sidecar racers. In one year, he literally won everything.

ROY: He ended up British champion didn't he?

ANN: Chris, Graham and Shelley used to spend every weekend running around in a field and doing whatever they wanted whilst the racing was on.

CHRIS: We stayed for holidays at each others houses right up until... when I was about fifteen, when Ken was of an age where he didn't want to get thrown off a bike all the time and started doing rallycross.

ANN: It was very close-knit wasn't it? You'd never worry about the kids.

ROY: No. They was all good kids.

JANE'S STORY 2

JANE: The police told us to get to the hospital as soon as possible. I asked what car had been in the accident and they said it was a blue BMW. Shelley had a blue BMW so I assumed... I just assumed it was her car.

The air ambulance was there and they were being cut out of the car. We just kind of dropped everything and headed off.

We must have been driving for twenty minutes or so and then... it... it kind of dawned on us, we didn't know what hospital we were going to. It was ludicrous! We phoned Aylesbury. They weren't expecting anybody. Then Milton Keynes said, "Yes we are expecting..." but they couldn't say anything more.

We hotfooted it to Milton Keynes... a long, silent journey. We were just... just thinking the worst...

We were kind of ushered through to a private room and the nurse sat us all down. He just told us that Shelley was in a poor way... preparing us really for what we were going to see... emphasising she'd suffered a very severe head injury. I really did not grasp what that entailed.

Then we went through and... there she was... laid out there. *(Voice cracking.)* She was on life support, a neck brace, on oxygen drips and all the rest of it. I just remember the smell of blood. Her clothes had been cut away, her eyes were half open and that was kind of scary, she was, you know, unconscious.

Danny just took one look and... he had to be taken away because he was just too distressed. You don't know what to do for the best do you? We were all fearing the worst I guess?

No one's really telling you... you're listening to phone conversations, to nurses talking... saying... the brain injury wasn't something they could treat at Milton Keynes. They didn't have a neurology department. I remember one thing... a nurse came across and said to me: "Insist... insist she goes to Oxford. She has to go to have any chance... you must insist. Even if she doesn't make it, you will know you did all you could for her."

That decision was made about one o'clock in the morning and we headed off to Oxford. Danny went home with Kayleigh to look after the dog and we kept him posted with what was going on. We went to get a toothbrush and followed the ambulance and when we got there just sat… sat waiting.

CHRIS: We stayed on Ken's team and being a bit older I was a bit more handy on the tools. We travelled all round Europe and of course it didn't cost anything. It was incredible really. Something not a lot of people've done… and we won a Dutch Championship!

ROY: Chris then started to get into these model racing cars.

CHRIS: Yeh, I wanted to race something myself… little petrol engine ones with two speed gearboxes… quite impressive! The first time me 'n' Dad went to watch… it was quite funny 'cos you'd hear them going down the straights, and it was like *(Very high pitched.)* meeeeeee *(Slightly less high-pitched.)* meeeeeee … and we'd go, "Are they changing gear?" I got into that. Then I got into it a bit heavier.

ROY: These little cars… were like a thousand quid each!

ANN: He was just throwing money at it.

CHRIS: But I was still little league.

ROY: It was big money!

CHRIS: We went to Staffordshire thinking we had the nuts of a setup. The world champion was there and they are… they're professionals… you know… you think what you've got is good, then you look at theirs and you think "We're nothing!" They'd be spending tens of thousands!

Just randomly through work, one of my friends started racing, you know, real cars at Matchams. I'd just passed my driving test so I said "I'll come and watch." and I thought "Yeh. That's do-able", not really knowing… you know… not really knowing about how much you could pick a car up for… so I got home, and… well we had a great big row about it!

ROY: Don't be so bloody daft! It'll cost too much!

CHRIS: You can pick them up for nothing.

ROY: You don't know enough about them. You'll have to buy a race seat, decent crash helmet, harness, rolling cage, window nets. Where are you gonna get all the money from? What happens if you crash?

CHRIS: To be quite truthful, Dad, I've already got the car. I'm picking it up in a couple of weeks.

ROY: Where you got the money from?

CHRIS: Sold all my radio controlled car stuff.

ROY: What?

CHRIS: Yeh.

ROY: It's not just racing them. You got to get the suspension tweaked, you don't know nothing about that!

CHRIS: Well, I'll learn.

I'd proper got the bit for this so I'd already arranged for someone to come round and buy all my gear. I didn't sell it for what it was worth… just what it'd cost me to start up racing. I also got a cheap trailer and took the car over to my dad's workshop. He was looking round it and was like:

ROY: Smart!

CHRIS: … and he ended up…

ROY: I could do this!

CHRIS: *(Laughing)* Within a week he'd bought a car!

ANN: I felt a bit bamboozled about the whole thing! I didn't have a lot to say about it, but, being the considerate and loving wife I was, I never got in their way!

ROY: Of course it really did get Chris and me close, I can see that. None of my other lads wanted to know… his brothers, you know, they weren't interested and he was just getting better and better… and winning as well!

JANE'S STORY 3

JANE: It was three o'clock in the morning. The neurosurgeons came out and sort of said… you know… they explained she'd been travelling at speed and hit a retaining wall… it's like her brain was rattled around inside her skull. All the nerves had been sheared. They just said, they didn't think she'd survive the next twenty-four hours. Twenty-four long, long hours. The neurosurgeon came out and said:

"It's one of the worst skull fractures I've seen. Take it from me, there's nothing you can do. The best thing is to go home and just relax. Go home. We'll call you when we need you."

You just sort of think… well there's no way we can go home.

I think he was trying to say, "Get yourself organised… keep thinking about something else because… when you're in the hospital you're just focused on what's going on there." I appreciate what he was saying but never in a million years would you do that. I just remember us walking round zombified. Anyway, each time the doctors came to see us it was… they just kept saying they didn't expect her to survive the next twenty-four hours.

Life as we knew it was falling apart, but we had to be strong for our girl who was battling to survive… and for our son.

CHRIS'S STORY 4

CHRIS: Incidentally… I met my wife Lucy at a race meeting. I recognised her from school and asked what she was doing there…

LUCY: Watching my brother.

CHRIS: Who's your brother?"

LUCY: Gary.

CHRIS: That ain't your brother?

LUCY: It is… "Gary, ain't you my brother?"

CHRIS: And I feel a right dick because he says: "Yeh". That's how we met… I must have been seventeen.

JANE: We stayed until we got to that twenty-four hour mark at one o'clock on Sunday morning. Then it started to be revealed that... that we wouldn't know until she was conscious what damage had been done... whether she'd be able to walk or talk... you know... what kind of life she'd have.

In our heads we were just thinking... it'll all fix... it'll all mend... it'll all get better again. It'll all be... it'll all be back to how it was.

We stayed the Sunday and Monday night and went home on Tuesday to get changed. They have, like a relative's room. They let you stay there the first night, but they don't like you to take advantage of it. They want you to find a local hotel to stay in because obviously there's new cases coming in all the time. I think Monday night we just slept rough in the waiting room... just kept moving about so the staff didn't find us *(Laughing.)* sort of waiting around the hospital because we just didn't want to be that far from her... you know. I was getting dug out to do bed baths... the intensive care nurses were brilliant, you know, they involve you to sort of... to care for her.

CHRIS'S STORY 5

CHRIS: In 2000, I went into 1300 stock cars, racing a Nova... front-wheel drive.

LUCY: No one had one back then.

CHRIS: Mine was the first one done... like we wanted to do something a bit radical. I spent a lot of money on that car... a lot of money I didn't really have. I was on a low wage. We'd just had Bryoni then... and it sounds weird... but, whatever your financial situation, you always find enough money to race. Lucy was brilliant on the money... our savings for a holiday, you know.

LUCY: On certain championships you'd win a bit of money...

CHRIS: I got interviewed on telly, for a program called Bangers and Smash, which was quite cool but I just kind of lost interest.

LUCY: They were trying to bring new blood into the sport and brought out this new formula... Rookies... where you could do it on a budget... literally race anything.

CHRIS: They decided to hold a world championship and I thought "I'll have a go at that!"

LUCY: There were 140 odd cars at the meeting.

CHRIS: *(Rubbing hands with glee)* £1,000 to the winner!

ROY: He was never expected to win. Never!

CHRIS: A lot of the big banger boys were doing it 'cos they thought it was easy to... you know...

ROY: It was quite comical.

ANN: I didn't go.

CHRIS: I won the heat... twenty-five quid...

That'll pay for the kebabs on the way home, Luce.

LUCY: It was quality and he qualified for the final.

CHRIS: They draw grid positions out of a hat.

LUCY: Chris came in number three!

CHRIS: I thought, "This is all right!"

ROY: Normal banger races are like ten or twelve laps.

LUCY: This was thirty!

CHRIS: I led it from about five laps in. Cars were just dwindling off and I'm thinking "I could win this!"

ROY: I'm stood at the finish line, and there was like twenty-five, thirty cars out there, and you don't know who's who… and a bloke stood near, knew me and I said to him:
"What is he… 'bout fourth is he?"
"Is he hell? He's winning it!"
"What?"

CHRIS: With about five laps to go… it was just in my head… I started thinking, "I can win this!" *(Laughing.)* I got a video of this race like… and you can see my dad… he runs up the straight then he'll come back down and… .

ROY: … for about five laps running up and down again and again… I was absolutely blooming knackered!

CHRIS: I started copping out on the final lap… hitting the wall, hitting parked cars, all sorts of things and I was thinking, "Oh watch me throw this away!"

LUCY: Yeh.

ROY: I couldn't believe it. But he won!

CHRIS: I went across the line punching the air and that…

ROY: He went over the line and his arms went up like that.

CHRIS: Then, on the slowdown lap I was thinking, "I'm world champion!"

LUCY: There were pound signs in my eyes!

ANN: The one meeting I don't go to and he wins it!

CHRIS: It was a complete surprise… completely unexpected. I was… I was… yeh… I'd never won anything big before and I won £1,000 cash! Didn't have it very long because someone (**LUCY** *holds her hand out.*) held their hand out for it. I held that title for a year and had a gold roof on my car whenever I was racing.

JANE: Thankfully for Shelley she didn't have, you know, facial scars, but her head was cut open from ear to ear so they could remove all the bits of... of the fractured skull erm... because they could pierce her oedema... once that's pierced it kills the brain tissue. Thankfully there was only a couple of areas where it had actually... sort of pierced it. We stayed the Sunday and Monday night and went home on Tuesday to change. On the Wednesday we were told the pressure was still building up and within the next twenty-four hours we could still lose her. We were going through the whole thing again. On Friday the neurosurgeon said they... they... the team had reached a decision to do a craniotomy... cutting away part of the skull to make room for the brain to swell. She went down for the operation at about five o'clock.

At ten they came through to say they thought it'd been successful but we'd know more in the morning. We stayed that night too.

Saturday morning everything was good, so we went home to get a change of clothes. John and Danny were still racing. I think it was their way of coping... you know, getting some kind of normality. Danny had racing commitments, he's a professional speedway racer...

When I got back to the hospital the intensive care staff were all... very down... you know. "What's wrong? What's happened?"

"She needs a blood transfusion but the anaesthetist is saying they're not going to give her any more blood because the situation has deteriorated. The doctor will have a word with you."

He just sort of... said that the operation had not been as successful as they'd hoped and they didn't think she'd get through the next twenty-four hours. He asked me if she'd talked about organ donation... and what were our feelings about it. He was basically telling me that... you know... prepare yourself... prepare yourself because this is the end.

I just... I just kept saying "You can't give up on her! There is still hope! There must be!"

And he was saying: "Even if she survives, her quality of life will be so poor, it won't be fair on her or your family."

I wouldn't believe it *(Crying)*. I phoned John and said, "You need to get... you need to come back and help."

We were all in disbelief really 'cos although Shelley was still unconscious, we'd... kind of got it into our heads that she was going to get better and everything was going to be fine, and now we had a whole new set of issues to deal with. She wasn't going to get better and if she did, she'd be severely disabled.

That night we stayed at the hospital waiting for the knock on the door to say she'd gone. *(Tearful.)* They wouldn't let me stay in intensive care. She could have died and we weren't there and you know... you just... anyway at seven o'clock in the morning I said: "Can I come through?" and Candice, one of the nurses who was looking after her, said: "Shelley's my little miracle... she'll get through." She was saying prayers for her.

Miraculously it had all changed. They said we're gonna pull all the stops out. I still wonder to this day if they... it's almost like a test on the parents. Will they see it through or walk away... say goodbye and give those organs to someone else?

That thought will never leave me.

THE ACCIDENT

CHRIS: In 2006 I'd got back in touch with Graham *(GRAHAM enters on his mobile phone texting. CHRIS indicates towards him)* again.

LUCY: He'd had this huge accident...

CHRIS: He was in Poole hospital 'cos it'd happened at Wimborne racetrack...

LUCY: He was racing with his dad... he was in a sidecar...

CHRIS: He'd broken his leg so, being near Southampton where I live, I went to see him. We hadn't seen each other since we were fifteen! That's how we first made contact. Then I'd give him a random text... and he told me his mum had died. I felt real bad for him. We got chatting and he said:

GRAHAM: Let's meet up.

CHRIS: It had to be a weekend when there was no racing for either of us... and we arranged it for Cup Final day, May 2007.

GRAHAM: I happened to see Shelley *(Indicates SHELLEY.)* the night before and she said:

SHELLEY: I'll be up for it!

GRAHAM: It'll be a laugh.

CHRIS: *(On mobile to GRAHAM.)* I've got an interview in the morning so I may be a bit later... say two-ish 'cos I'll have to change. Don't want to be coming up, all posh in my suit!

GRAHAM: Okay. Come to mine, then we'll go to the pub for the Cup Final.

CHRIS: Oh yeh. Man U. Still a fan?

GRAHAM: That'll never change.

LUCY: He got the job.

CHRIS: I was buzzing! Earning a lot more money and a company car.

LUCY: He was saying...

CHRIS: I haven't got time to talk now babe, I've got to get changed and off!

LUCY: Alright, bye!

CHRIS: Talk more later. *(He rushes off.)*

LUCY: Everything'd fallen into place perfectly. He wanted to progress to a higher formula. Now we could afford to.

CHRIS: I drove up to Graham's little village, Wing, just outside Milton Keynes.
(They meet.)
(Disparagingly.) I remember Graham had his Man U top on.

GRAHAM: That's where you'll be sleeping.

CHRIS: I dumped my bags in his room, had a real quick... actually, I don't think we even had a cup of tea! We jumped in his car and drove to the local. It was a sunny day... a nice day. You know, meeting up with... I really considered him as possibly one of my best ever friends... really did... I grew up with him and was as close to him as to school friends who I'd see every day and... yeh and it was all going...

GRAHAM: We was playing pool. Chris was getting on with everyone and we was all having a good laugh.

CHRIS: There was a nipper working in there... working behind the bar, called Korsh and I remembered him... and then Shelley turned up.
*(***SHELLEY*** enters.)*
She was a PE teacher or an assistant or something. She called the netball team "her girls". I remember her saying:

SHELLEY: My girls are doing well at netball.

GRAHAM: My friend was leaving for Australia the next day so there was a surprise party. We said we'd go back to my house, get ready, then we'll go sort of thing.

CHRIS: I wasn't too keen. I remember feeling a bit... "Oh, I ain't gonna know anyone", so I said something to Shelley:

SHELLEY: I'll come too. We've got catching up to do.

CHRIS: Cool!
The match finished. To my knowledge no one had drunk anything other than cokes. I know for a fact, if Graham'd been drinking I wouldn't have got in the car.

GRAHAM: No one had been drinking. I'm certain of that. I mean, a couple of shandies… I remember being offered a third and I turned it down, I didn't want to be silly. I'd have one later on… save it… save it for later.

I drove back to my house and we got changed. Shelley left her car at the pub.

CHRIS: They both had blue BMWs… hers was the standard one…

SHELLEY: His, the more powerful M3.

GRAHAM: I released the alarm button and Shelley said:

SHELLEY: Is it all right if I drive?

GRAHAM: I think I umm'd and ah'd.

CHRIS: There wasn't a moment's hesitation… there wasn't even an "Oh well." All I can think of now is that bit in *Too Much Punch for Judy*, "Okay then… you drive" and the keys being thrown… 'cos it was a throw of the keys.

GRAHAM: I trusted her and she had an interest. We stood either side of the car with the key in the door and it was just like… "Go on then. But look. Don't forget… it is powerful."

Chris was cool about it.

CHRIS: It wasn't like she was going from a little Fiesta to a BMW.

GRAHAM: I went round to the passenger side and she got in to drive. I have no idea why, I'd never let anyone drive my car before.

CHRIS: There's not much room in the back of the BMW – three door. I was sat with my leg up and wasn't belted in.

GRAHAM: I didn't wear one either…

CHRIS: I don't ever wear one… like, I've never been hurt on the track so why on the roads when you're driving at thirty miles an hour! I got stopped once by the police for not having one on and as shit luck would have it, my mum was driving down the same road and stopped behind us.

ANN: What's up?

CHRIS: "I wasn't wearing my seat belt." She'll tell you this… she actually said to the copper:

ANN: I don't understand it! He races cars and he has to strap himself into a five-point seat belt. I don't understand why he won't put them on!

CHRIS: I got fined.

I didn't wear a seat belt whether I was in the front or the back. I'm quite open about it. I do now though!

GRAHAM: Shelley sat in the driver's seat and I described to her how to move the seat forward.

SHELLEY: Graham... don't worry. Everything's fine!

GRAHAM: The last thing I remember is pulling out of my drive and that's it. The drive was like a track... three quarters of a mile long. I don't remember coming to the main road or anything...

CHRIS: I seem to... I couldn't at the time... but I seem to remember now because... obviously there's an accent from that sort of way and, clear as day... I remember exactly how Graham speaks. His exact words were:

GRAHAM: Steady on, Shell!

CHRIS: I'd like to think I was going off my head too...

POLICE: The road is subject to a thirty mile an hour speed limit, with clear thirty mile an hour signs on both sides of the road as you enter the village some 172 metres prior to the collision.

GRAHAM: Bloody hell Shelley, slow down!

POLICE: The road surface was in good condition.

CHRIS: It pisses me off to think I didn't say anything.

POLICE: Visibility was good for the speed limit.

JANE: Witnesses told the police that she'd overtaken a vehicle at speed...

WITNESS: I saw a VW go past at a sensible speed but was then aware of the sound of a racing engine. A dark blue BMW came into view at about ninety miles per hour.

ANN: *(Shaking head in disbelief.)* Ninety miles an hour...

POLICE: 122 metres prior to the bend, there are two warning signs. The BMW would not remain in its own lane whilst negotiating the left hand bend at this speed.

JANE: She lost control as it caught the back end of an oncoming vehicle.

ROY: It's very lucky that the bit they hit was behind the driver's door.

JANE: She'd've had no control of the car whatsoever.

ANN: They went into a fifteen foot brick wall...

JANE: ... a garden retainer wall

ROY: ... with... like... sort of eight foot of dirt behind the wall and no give in it.

JANE: They went up the wall on their side at fifty miles an hour or so...

ANN: The roof buckled and stopped them being thrown out of the windscreen.

JANE: Shelley's head hit the window posts and crushed her skull. Seat belts would have stopped that.

ROY: The car bounced off the wall and landed like twenty, thirty foot over to the left.

POLICE: I arrived on the scene at 19:27 hours. The road surface was dry. The sun was shining on my arrival but would have been shining over the right shoulder of the BMW driver, so not a factor in this collision. The front offside of the BMW collided with the offside of the oncoming Renault, on the rear wing and offside wheel. The impact tore the Renault's wheel and axle from its mountings. The Renault yawned clockwise and came to rest facing the opposite direction to which it was travelling.

The condition of the tyres was not a factor in this collision. The minimum speed range of the BMW at the point of its collision with the Renault is between seventy and ninety-nine mph. The damage to the BMW, in my opinion, was created by an impact with the wall of between forty and fifty mph. There were no mechanical defects that would have been contributory to the collision. The occupants of the BMW were not wearing seat belts.

The driver of the Renault said in his statement:

DRIVER: I left work at about 18.30 and was heading home. I've travelled on this road five times a week in both directions over the last month. I was in my own car and am always careful to observe the speed limit in this kind of environment. I guess I was on the entry to the bend adjacent to the wall when I saw the blue car. It was in the outer extremity of its lane entering the bend. My instant reaction was: "Shit! That's fast." The vehicle seemed to be drifting into my lane on the bend. I didn't react because I had no chance to. It happened so fast. The blue car hit me. I remember hearing the bang like a loud firework. I don't recall my car spinning. My next recollection was being stationary on my side of the road but facing the wrong way. I put the handbrake on and tried to get out but couldn't, so climbed out of the passenger door. I recall someone asking me if I was alright. It took a few moments for me to get my bearings. I went to the blue car to help but there were so many people trying to get the occupants out that I came away. Remarkably, apart from a stiff neck, I was unhurt. I was very lucky!

LUCY: By chance, Graham's uncle Peter come up the road and recognised the number plate. He phoned Graham's sister and she come to the site and then, bless her, she informed everyone.

ROY: Ann had gone to bingo with Lucy and I was sat here, and about…

ANN: *(Laughing.)* You'd fallen asleep.

ROY: *(Laughs.)* Yeh. So about half past seven I was woke up… "This is the police from Milton Keynes." I just thought the worst straightaway. They said: "I'm sorry to tell you, but your son's had a bad accident. There were three of them in the car. All three are hurt and in hospital."

ANN: Where he'd been asleep he thought, "Did I hear that right" so he phoned the hospital …

ROY: … and they said "He's hurt… I can't say any more than that." I spoke to him and he could only just about talk.

ANN: … and at the end of the call you told me he said…

ROY: "I love you, Dad."

ANN: That's something else that makes you…

ROY: … so of course with that I went over to the Bingo place and said…

ANN: You tried my phone first. I remember Lucy saying…

LUCY: Your phone's ringing, Mum. I can feel it vibrating through my leg.

ANN: I looked at my phone: "It's Dad! He knows I can't answer the phone, stupid idiot!"

I put it back in my pocket. *(Laughter.)*

He phoned a couple of times and about five, ten minutes later, after they'd finished a game erm, the caller said:

"Is there a Mrs Gilfoy here?"

Lucy and I looked at each other:

LUCY: Put yer hand up, Mum!"

ANN: She said, "Can you go out to book sales?" *(**ANN** stands and moves towards **ROY**.)* Roy was stood there. I knew instantly, something was wrong.

LUCY: Mum said we needed to go. I knew either something had happened to Bryoni or Chris. When we come outside the bingo hall is when she turned round and said:

ANN: Chris's been involved in a car accident. He's broken his arm and his leg...

BRYONI: My cousin was babysitting me at our flat, then all of a sudden... we was just watching telly and all of a sudden Mum was just banging on the door and like, screaming, crying sort of thing and I was like trying to help... and I was "What's up, what's up?"

LUCY: Dad's been in a car accident... but he's gonna be alright.

BRYONI: What happened?

LUCY: We don't know, he's in hospital. It wasn't him driving and it wasn't his fault. He'll be all right... he's just broke some bones.

BRYONI: I want to see him.

LUCY: Not a good idea love... not just at the moment.

BRYONI: I was scared, sat on the sofa 'cos Mum was just running around getting things, saying Mum and Granddad were in the car downstairs. My cousin didn't know what to do, she was crying too. I was just sat on the couch.

LUCY: I phoned my mum in a blind panic and she took Bry.

BRYONI: It was really scary. *(Exits.)*

ANN: We didn't have a clue where to go. It would have been much better... far easier to go straight up the A34.

ROY: We went on the M1 and bugger me if they didn't... they didn't have two lanes shut down and there was a traffic jam.

ANN: We didn't get up there till twelve o'clock, having left at eight thirty!

ROY: We were just stuck in traffic and I said... I just said... "Bloody hell!"

ANN: Graham's sister is waiting for us in the car park. We've known the family for a long time and she warned us it wasn't a pretty sight.

ROY: As we walked through the doors Shelley was in the first room, and of course she was serious...

ANN: They wouldn't even let her mum and dad in. As we came in Jane looked up to me and she said:

JANE: Hallo, Ann. Kids, eh?

ANN: They said they were just turning Chris over so we had to wait outside. He was screaming wasn't he?

ROY: Yeah.

ANN: Awful screaming.

ROY: We could hear him but not see him.

ANN: I just wanted to go in there and smack 'em in the mouth 'cos they were hurting my son, you know. When they moved the blinds back it just churns you up. He was just laid there virtually erm... indescribable... you know... being your child.

ROY: He was an animal that's what it was.

LUCY: On the trolley, it was just a load of blood and mess laid there. It wasn't Chris, though I knew it was.

ANN: His clothes were all bloody in the corner, on the floor, where they'd cut them off.

ROY: There was blood everywhere... all on the floor and... and Chris had a mighty gash in his face... about two inches long down the temple, so that's how close it was.

LUCY: There were no doctors or nurses to tell us what was going on... what the injuries were or nothing.

ANN: They were all working on Shelley.

ROY: We didn't see her but we knew it was serious.

ANN: That's why Chris and Graham were in this room and nobody with them.

LUCY: His face was like sooo swollen.

ROY: The whole of his face

LUCY: He was unrecognisable.

ANN: His eyes were like golf balls.

ROY: He'd been thrown forward and hit the back of Shelley's seat.

25

LUCY: Both him and Graham were covered in her hair.

ROY: Nothing prepared us for this. Frightening! Frightening to see like, you know… we watch it on the telly but…

ANN: He had a big patch over the cuts on his face, some sort of… his leg was like in… there's a name for it… I can't remember… It was like erm… and it hung over the bed… and his arm… he had a plaster all over his arm there. He looked in a really sorry state.

LUCY: I'd thought he'd be sat up waiting to be plastered and then come straight home. All we could hear was the machines keeping Shelley alive. It was quite daunting.

ANN: His two eyes were sort of bluey, mauvey, blacky, awful! Erm… he looked at Lucy, and he looked at us, and he said, "I'm sorry." And that meant I'm sorry to put you through all of this.

LUCY: Were you wearing seat belts?

ANN: He said no.

LUCY: None of you?

ANN: He said no again.

LUCY: For fuck's sake! What a bunch of idiots you are! Can't you hear them machines! She's in serious trouble you know! *(Goes to leave but is calmed by* **ANN**.*)*

ANN: She just walked out. I walked out after her… I just said to her: "He needs us. It's a bit of a shock but we've got to get through this." She had a bit of a cry and came back in, what have you, and then she became very strong, didn't she?

ROY: Yeh.

ANN: Very strong for him..

LUCY: Instincts kick in and you don't worry.

ANN: One of the policemen said, off the record, that perhaps… if he'd been wearing a seatbelt he may well have broken his neck and not have survived… I'm not sure if he's right… but it was said.

LUCY: It's a strange feeling to know that someone beside you might not live past two o'clock unless something is done about it.

ANN: The only thing that separated Chris and Graham from Shelley was a curtain, so you could hear a lot of what was going on… you can work it out.

ROY: When we asked, all we really got was she's very, very poorly.

ANN: They didn't think she'd survive…

ROY: We've all been involved in racing, had friends badly… badly hurt… in wheelchairs… killed… so we're all sort of quite… but when it's our own… you know and it's… it's a real wannit? It's bloody horrible!

ANN: The next day we started to ask Chris about it. He couldn't remember.

ROY: He was dead blank.

ANN: I wanted to see where it'd happened. Graham's uncle took us…

ROY: Yeh that's right.

ANN: Andy took us.

ROY: Andy took us, yeh.

ANN: It was harrowing.

ROY: Have you seen the photos?[2] You've got to see them, that is… erm… when you see the car it's just unreal.

(Photos.)

LUCY: Graham had a bleed on the brain, broken ankle and a broken jaw. In the morning Chris had to have a plate put in for his femur, which was broken, and he'd also broken his humerus… that had to be plated. We stayed at a local hotel. None of us slept. We was up all night and then back at the hospital for about eight in the morning, waiting 'cos he'd already gone down to the theatre by then to have all the plates and that put in.
It was just a waiting game.

I think, all in all, we was down there for about seven hours, wannit?

CHRIS: *(Entering in a wheel chair.)* I was thinking, alright people break their legs… six weeks. I'll be all right. I probably look a bit beat up. Then she took the photo and showed me.

(Photo.)

2   The photos referred to in this and other scenes are available for use in performances of the play only. For details contact info@salamanderstreet.com.

I thought… "Christ!"

Then I asked about Shelley and it hit home to me.

I went through a stage of uncontrollable crying and just… I'd be sat there and we'd be having a conversation just about general stuff, the weather or the news and I'd be there and… I'd go in… like a split second I might be out of the conversation, and I'd be sat crying and not know why. It was crazy. Talking, then breaking down in tears. It went on for weeks. Very strange. Weird feeling.

LUCY: Within two days they had you up and walking. *(She helps him up.)* They wanted you out of bed.

CHRIS: I was a bit cheesed off because I was up there, and of course none of my mates could come and see me, and the only person there was Luce and she was having a hard time of it… was only allowed in at certain times and it was… it wasn't nice. Once Shelley went off to Oxford we didn't hear much more about her.

LUCY: Graham was moved to Stoke Mandeville.

CHRIS: He was really on the mend… really quickly 'n' all.

GRAHAM: Although I recovered quickly, it felt like I'd been beaten to death sort of thing. I kept having dizzy spells, like I'd been in a giant hamster ball and pushed about. My back was like… I was in agony with it and… and I lost everything.

I was renting the place we went to get changed in and, while I was in hospital, the guy got my stuff and threw it in a barn. He just didn't want me living there no more. He took advantage of me being… there was a rumour going about that we'd all been killed and… he kicked me out basically, so I had no… when I come out of hospital… I was there for two weeks… my Nan turned up and she said: "You're coming to live with me." She took me in and sort of built me my mind and strength up again.

Eight weeks on and I lost my job. I just couldn't do it no more 'cos I had no feeling in my hand. I was a ground worker so, being a hands- on job, I just thought… we sort of mutually agreed that I'd lose my job basically. That was after about eight weeks.

I had an invite from my friend who was a professional speedway rider to go live with him and mechanic for him in the Isle of Wight which I did for nearly two years

I lost the car as well 'cos... well, I didn't think about the insurance issue when I let Shelley drive. I come away with nothing. It was a life-changing experience, an eye opener to how things can suddenly change. We were lucky we was in a BMW really. They said if it'd been, like, a smaller car we'd have been killed.

I'm a great believer in things happening for a reason. I'd lost my mum exactly two months before that accident. She was only forty-eight when she died and erm, I sort of went off the rails a little bit. It sort of come to a climax with the car accident and then, after that I just... yeh, different view on life itself... different perspective. I nearly died, nearly lost my life and I don't want to... I've still got plenty of time left. Yeh... everything happens for a reason... to tell me to stop doing... like a warning ... if I'd have carried on I'd probably have ended up worse. All I was interested in was women, drink, drugs... and yeh... just putting everything to the back of my mind basically. I don't do none of that now.

I stopped smoking, got fitter... and... I've got a different view on life. I cycle and go to the gym for my fitness, to be as successful as I can be at my age. I'm now settled down with my lovely girlfriend, Charlotte, my doggie Doug and Charlotte's three children !

I still have visible scars from the accident. I still have no feeling in two fingers on my left hand from the accident.

It's devastating what's happened to Chris and Shelley.

At first it was too much of a reminder on my part... seeing Chris struggle to get his leg right... it was like, hard, real hard seeing him like that but now I'm in regular contact with them both. I'd seen Shelley a few times at race meetings but last summer, thirteen years after the accident, we all met up at a motorsport meeting. It was the first time we'd been together since the accident! It always great to see Shelley... I give her a huge hug as if to say: "Thank God you're still here."

CHRIS: After a week in Milton Keynes I went off for what was to be a long stay, near home, in the Southampton General.

BRYONI: When I saw him it wasn't my dad. It didn't look like him. Obviously you knew it was him but... he was just... I gave him a hug and then like, "What's going on?" It was really strange seeing him like that. We had to live with my grandparents... Dad's mum 'n' dad... we were there for about six months... the three of us, 'cos Dad couldn't get up and down the stairs and toilet and stuff properly.

LUCY: He had fourteen operations between 2007 and 2014.

CHRIS: Metal plates are in two parts of my arm. They'll stay with me forever. My leg's been the main problem though. I've had multiple procedures...

LUCY: Many of which didn't work.

CHRIS: I still have broken parts of metal in my femur from the last operation...

LUCY: ... which they classed as successful!

ANN: His right leg is still, and will always be, in constant pain.

CHRIS: There's still a high chance it'll be amputated....

ROY: It has a substantial impact on his day to day living...

LUCY: ... taking the full quota of painkillers every day.

CHRIS: The accident changed everything. Not only my life; Lucy's, Mum and Dad's and friends' lives. Everyone I'm in connection with. It's affected everyone. Like, we had to move. Lucy had to give up work, so there's a financial struggle as well. It was going from doing everything to not being able to feed yourself or wipe my arse, you know. Had to get the nurse to do it, or Lucy. That's not nice, it's degrading.

LUCY: You and Bryoni used to go out...

CHRIS: Yeh. If I were going somewhere I'd say, "Coming, Bry?"

LUCY: That all stopped, didn't it? She's been pushed from pillar to post. If you've got hospital, she's pushed off to stay with my mum or yours, or pushed off to her friends. As much as she doesn't mind...

CHRIS: I'd hate to know the long-term effect it's had on her. You know what I mean?

BRYONI: I don't remember Dad much before the accident. To me he's always walked with a limp or with crutches when it hurts, or... sort of thing... like, he's only just gone back to work after six or seven years.

CHRIS: I still dream about the accident sometimes... like the thing of... of saying... of asking Shelley to slow down... stuff like that. My dreams seem to be trying to fill gaps in the story.

I've been in a very bad place... I don't know if it's suicidal as such but... really down and... you know...

LUCY: Constant tears, constant moaning, constant jumping at everybody. You can't say nothing, else you'd jump down their throats wouldn't ya? Even your dad. You were really horrible.

CHRIS: A few years have passed since we did those interviews and... well I don't want it to be all doom and gloom. It isn't. The play has been amazing. It upsets me when I watch it but that's good, it means it's doing it's job. I actually love watching it and meeting the cast and so on... but best of all there's Bry...

She came home from school one day... she was only ten, and said...

BRYONI: Dad, can I race at Cheetah's?

CHRIS: I was absolutely speechless! Cheetah's was the local dirt track which was a great breeding ground for junior racers.

BRYONI: Dad! Don't stand there narrating! He still never misses the chance to do a good bit of acting!

Well?

CHRIS: Yeh, course you can... but I don't want it to be a flash in the pan thing. If you're doing it you'll do it properly!

BRYONI: Let's do it.

CHRIS: Within a week I had a car ready for her.

BRYONI: He did!

LUCY: She took to it like a duck to water winning junior races all over the country.

CHRIS: When she was sixteen...

LUCY:　　... in her first year in the adult banger racing division...

CHRIS/LUCY: She won the Ladies Championship...

CHRIS: Youngest ever to win it.

CHRIS & LUCY: We were gobsmacked!

BRYONI: Why?

LUCY: She then went on to silence the doubters...

CHRIS: … who said it was beginner's luck to win again the following season.

LUCY: First person to retain the title!

CHRIS: Since then she has moved on to racing with men and has had some good results!

BRYONI: Say about the transit…

LUCY: Yeh. She even raced…

ALL 3: A transit van! *(They laugh.)*

CHRIS: *(Slowing the pace again.)* Things haven't really changed for Shelley though. We have met up and still message each other all the time on Facebook and by text. It was always, "Hi, how are you?" etc etc. One day a message popped up. It was from Shelley and out of the blue. The one line on the message said: "Do u blame me?"

I was in complete shock! I mean, if you cut all the airs and graces out then yes, she was driving and it wouldn't have happened if she wasn't going so fast. You can't dust around that, but she has suffered immensely and will do for the rest of her life, so no, I don't blame her. She's got the raw end of the deal. She's had it bad and, on a positive note, whatever state we're in… at least we're all still here.

JANE'S STORY 6

JANE: Shelley went into hospital that Saturday, May 19th 2007 and didn't return home full time for another three years. The Shelley that went out with her friends that day was not the same girl who came home from hospital.

For two months she was in a coma and it's not like the movies. You don't wake up and everything is fine and dandy. When Shelley woke up she couldn't walk, couldn't talk, couldn't eat, didn't know who we were, had to wear nappies, had to be fed. She was literally like a baby again.

I was concerned about Graham but felt he was being taken care of, but I did feel guilty about Chris. Poor Chris. I was so tied up with Shelley in the hospital that I didn't pay a great deal of attention to him. You know, I'd ask on Facebook and we saw him at Speedway 'cos he came to watch Danny race in Bournemouth. He was still on crutches and that was probably three years after and I just thought, "Oh my God… he's had as bad a time of it as we have… and he's like, a father… his home and his social life.

I wouldn't wish what we went through as a family on anyone. This crash could have been prevented if Shelley had not been driving so fast. Her injuries would not have been so severe if she had been wearing a seat belt. Although Shelley had fully comprehensive insurance, she was under twenty-five and therefore not insured to drive another person's vehicle. Thankfully, she does now recognise us again, has learned to walk, and talk… but her life has changed drastically.

Shelley is managing the Tea Room at our Nursery (which continues to flourish) and has a whole host of surrogate nans and grandads (customers) who all love her drive her mad!! Shelley completed the Super Hero Triathlon event last August which was a major accomplishment.

(A film[3] is shown of the real **SHELLEY** *saying the following.)*

SHELLEY: Hello, my name is Shelley. I'm twenty-nine. When I was twenty-three I was footloose and fancy-free. I didn't ask for the car crash, but I didn't prevent it.

Doctors didn't think I would make it, but I'm here now talking to you. I used to be a very good netball player. Those days are gone now.

3 https://www.youtube.com/watch?v=kEW3lRxEgVo

I hope to play again one day. There are days when I feel like starting again. I wish I could, but I can't. That's life, I suppose.

There is more to life than driving a fast car.

I know that now.

Every day is a struggle but I get there... just!

Digital Resources for Teachers

There are a number of practical digital resources for teachers and students who are studying *Chequered Flags to Chequered Futures* as a set text.

A video recording is also available for download – please see the *Chequered Flags to Chequered Futures* page on www.salamanderstreet.com for further details.

Chequered Flags to Chequered Futures DVD/Download

Presented by Victoria Shanghai Academy in Hong Kong who commissioned it.

Mark describes *Chequered Flags* as his most mature verbatim RTA play with a fascinating structure and some amazingly powerful monologues for a female performer. Also, a Q & A with playwright Mark Wheeller, the director, Joanna Crimmins and the Gilfoy family (central characters in the play). Chris Gilfoy developed the role of Chris in the original production of *Chicken*.

Chequered Flags to Chequered Futures is available as part of the DVD of *Chicken!* performed by StopWatch Theatre in Education Company (Professional TIE Company)

Available from Salamander Street.

Teachers – if you are interested in buying a set of texts
for your class please email info@salamanderstreet.com
– we would be happy to discuss discounts and keep you up
to date with our latest publications and study guides.

Missing Dan Nolan
Paperback 9781913630287
eBook 9781913630294

Chicken!
Paperback 9781913630331
eBook 9781913630324

Game Over
Paperback 9781913630263
eBook 9781913630270

Hard to Swallow
Paperback 9781913630249
eBook 9781913630256

Too Much Punch For Judy
Paperback 9781913630300
eBook 9781913630317

Hard to Swallow, Easy to Digest
(with Karen Latto)
Paperback 9781913630409
eBook 9781913630393

Hard to Swallow, Easy to Digest: Student Workbook
Paperback 9781913630416
eBook 9781913630423

The Story Behind … Too Much Punch for Judy
Paperback 9781913630379
eBook 9781913630386

Salamander Street will be publishing new editions of Mark's plays
in 2020 – follow us on Twitter or Facebook or visit our website for the
latest news.

www.salamanderstreet.com